W9-CAG-588

be happy.

A little book to help you
live a happy life.

by Monica Sheehan

RUNNING PRESS
PHILADELPHIA

For Andrew Kroon

We love you always.

Running Press
Hachette Book Group
1290 Avenue of the Americas, New York, NY 10104
www.runningpress.com
@Running_Press

Printed in China

Originally published in hardcover by Running Press in March 2007

First Deluxe Edition: August 2018

Published by Running Press, an imprint of Perseus Books, LLC, a subsidiary
of Hachette Book Group, Inc. The Running Press name and logo is
a trademark of the Hachette Book Group.

The Hachette Speakers Bureau provides a wide range of authors for speaking event
To find out more, go to www.hachettespeakersbureau.com
or call (866) 376-6591.

The publisher is not responsible for websites (or their content)
that are not owned by the publisher.

Cover illustration, interior illustrations, and print book design by Monica Sheehan.

Library of Congress Control Number: 2006930239

ISBNs: 978-0-7624-6497-5 (deluxe hardcover), 978-0-7624-6498-2 (ebook),
978-0-7624-2962-2 (original hardcover)

RRD-S

10 9 8 7 6 5 4 3 2 1

merci. gracias. thank you.

to all the people who helped
make this new edition possible.

Kristin Kiser
Jess & Frances
Jon Anderson
Brian Murphy
Bob & Chelsea
Gary Louris
Jen & Leigh
Sheila & Eddie McCrossin
and from 'the Sheehan tribe'
Kara, Jack & Meredith!
Andrew, Eamon & Emmet
Nora, Sarah & Stephen
...and last but not least
Saint Annie & Georgio!

Show up.

Follow your heart.

Stay inspired.

Stop being a victim.

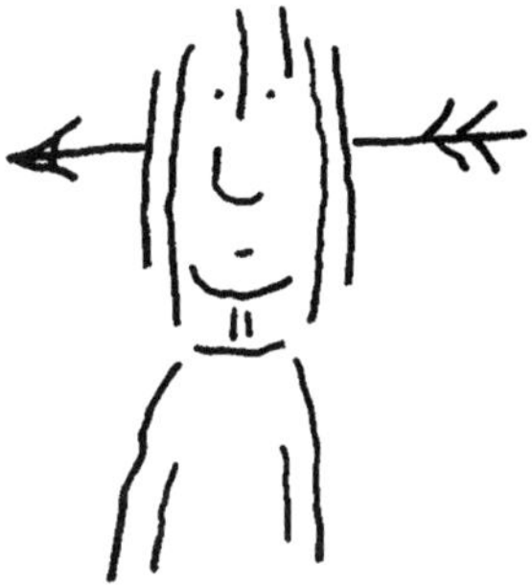

Do things you're
good at.

Love your work.

Have a sense
of wonder.

Don't isolate.

Find people
you love.

Set goals.

Finish what
you started.

TAP
TAP

Help others.

Do a one day
news fast.

Dance.

Pamper yourself.

Face your fears.

Limit television.

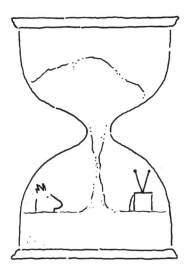

Go to a museum.

Exercise.

Any decision is better
than no decision.

Clear the clutter.

Unplug.

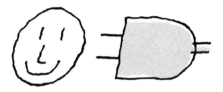

Recharge.

Listen to music.

Get in touch
with nature.

Lighten up.

Reach out.

Get a good
night's sleep.

Have a moral compass.

Read books.

Buy yourself flowers.

Set up a
realistic schedule.

Don't compare yourself with others.

Live in the moment.

PAST | FUTURE

Every night reflect
on the 'good' things
about your day.

Don't beat
yourself up.

Let go.

Accept that life
has its
ups and downs.

Get a new
perspective.

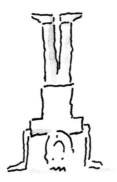

Value who you are
right now.

Don't focus on
negative thoughts.

Focus on creating
what you desire.

Be open to
new ideas.

Be kind.

Let people know
how special they are.

Make time just
to have fun.

Be honest
with yourself.

Say thank you to the people
who teach you, support you,
encourage you,

and get you
a cup of coffee.

Don't forget...
money doesn't
buy happiness.

Give away what you
don't need,
to someone who does.

Be part of
a community.

Make a
gratitude list.

Love your Mother Earth.

Be strong.

Believe in yourself.

Do your best.

PRETTY GOOD

PERSONAL BEST

GETTING BY

Don't lose hope.

(You never know what
tomorrow will bring.)

TODAY

TOMORROW

Keep learning.

Want what
you have.

Believe in something bigger than yourself.

Stay close to
friends and family

(or friends that
are your family).

Be true to yourself.

My Gratitude List:

_____

_____

_____

_____

_____

_____

_____

_____

_____

_____

_____

My Goals:

_____

_____

_____

_____

_____

_____

_____

_____

_____

_____

_____

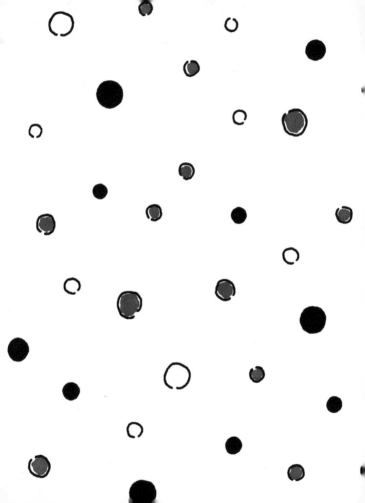